Big Rocks,

Written by Margie Burton, Cathy French, and Tammy Jones

You can look for rocks everywhere. Some rocks are big and some are little.

Here is a big rock on
the moon. The moon is
made of rocks.

These rocks are very,
very little.

This hole was made from a big rock. It came down from the sky.

This little rock is old.
It has a leaf print on it.

These little rocks are old, too.

These rocks are tools.

This big rock is made
of layers of rock. The oldest rock is
down at the bottom.

This big rock was made from fire.
It came out of a volcano.

This big rock is made of mud. You can scratch and write on it.

This rock is made from little rocks set down by the wind.

You can take a little piece of this big rock and write with it.

This big wall is made of many kinds of small rocks. You can walk on it.

This big building is made of many kinds of rocks.

These big rocks are
in a cave.

This is the biggest
rock of all.